FABULOUS FLOWERS

The Gift of Colouring for Grown-ups

Michael O'Mara Books Limited

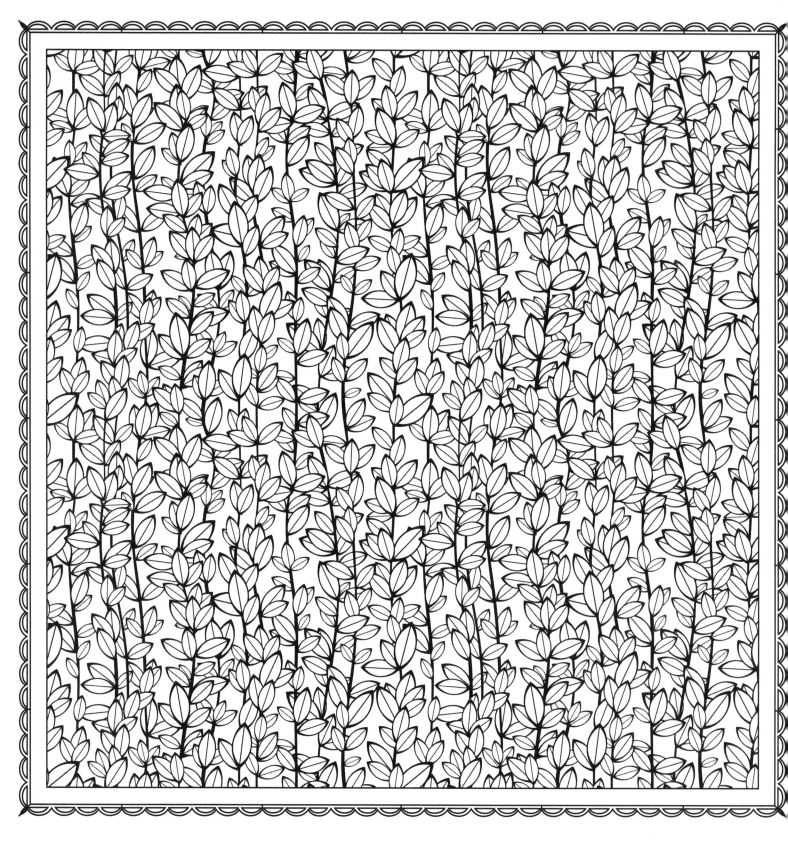

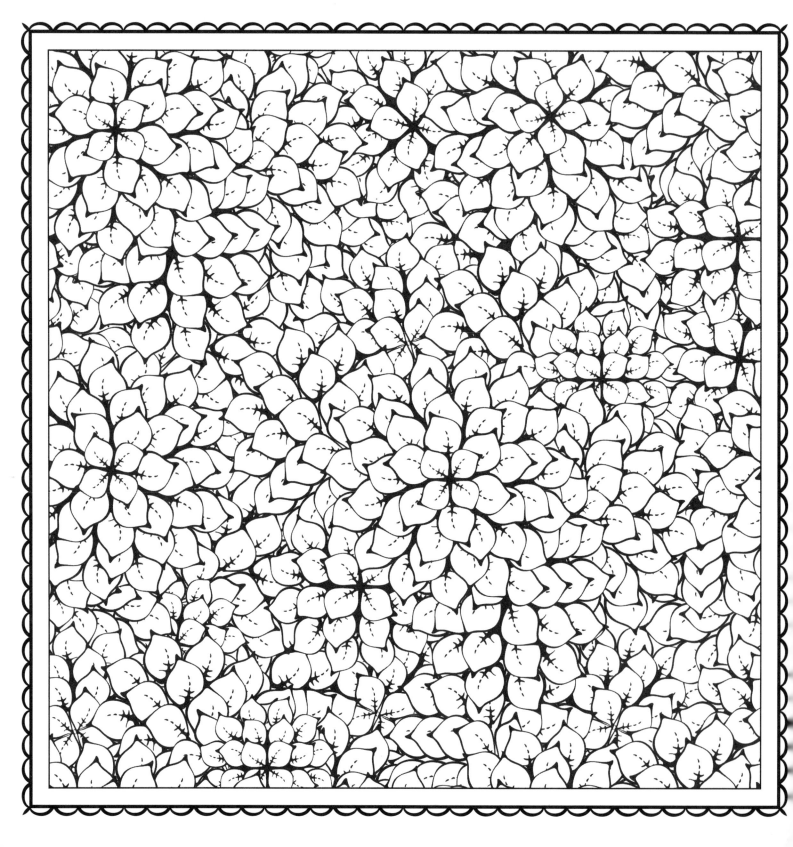

First published in Germany in 2014 by arsEdition GmbH, München.
This edition published in Great Britain in 2014 by Michael O'Mara Books Limited
9 Lion Yard, Tremadoc Road, London SW4 7NQ

A CIP catalogue record for this book is available from the British Library.

Papers used by Michael O'Mara Books Limited are natural, recyclable products made from wood grown in sustainable forests. The manufacturing processes conform to the environmental regulations of the country of origin.

ISBN: 978-1-78243-342-2

2 3 4 5 6 7 8 9 10

W www.mombooks.com   f Michael O'Mara Books   @OMaraBooks

Designed by Grafisches Atelier, arsEdition
Illustrations: Getty Images/Thinkstock
Colourization by Grafisches Atelier, Lea John

This book was printed in May 2015 by
UAB BALTO print, Utenos 41A, Vilnius LT-08217, Lithuania.